# Geometric shapes
# and
# Patterns
## Coloring book

50 creative design
Relaxing and Stress relief

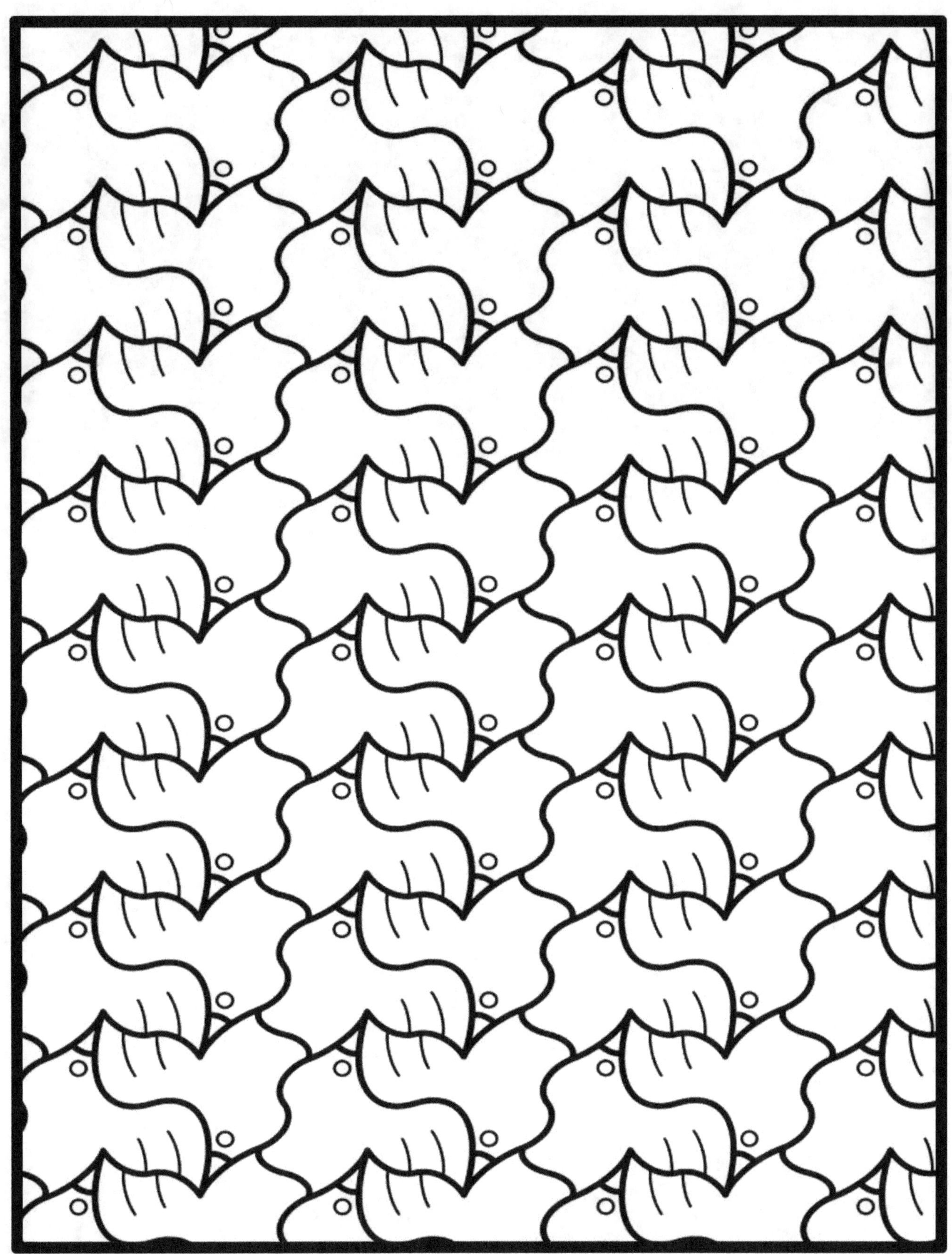

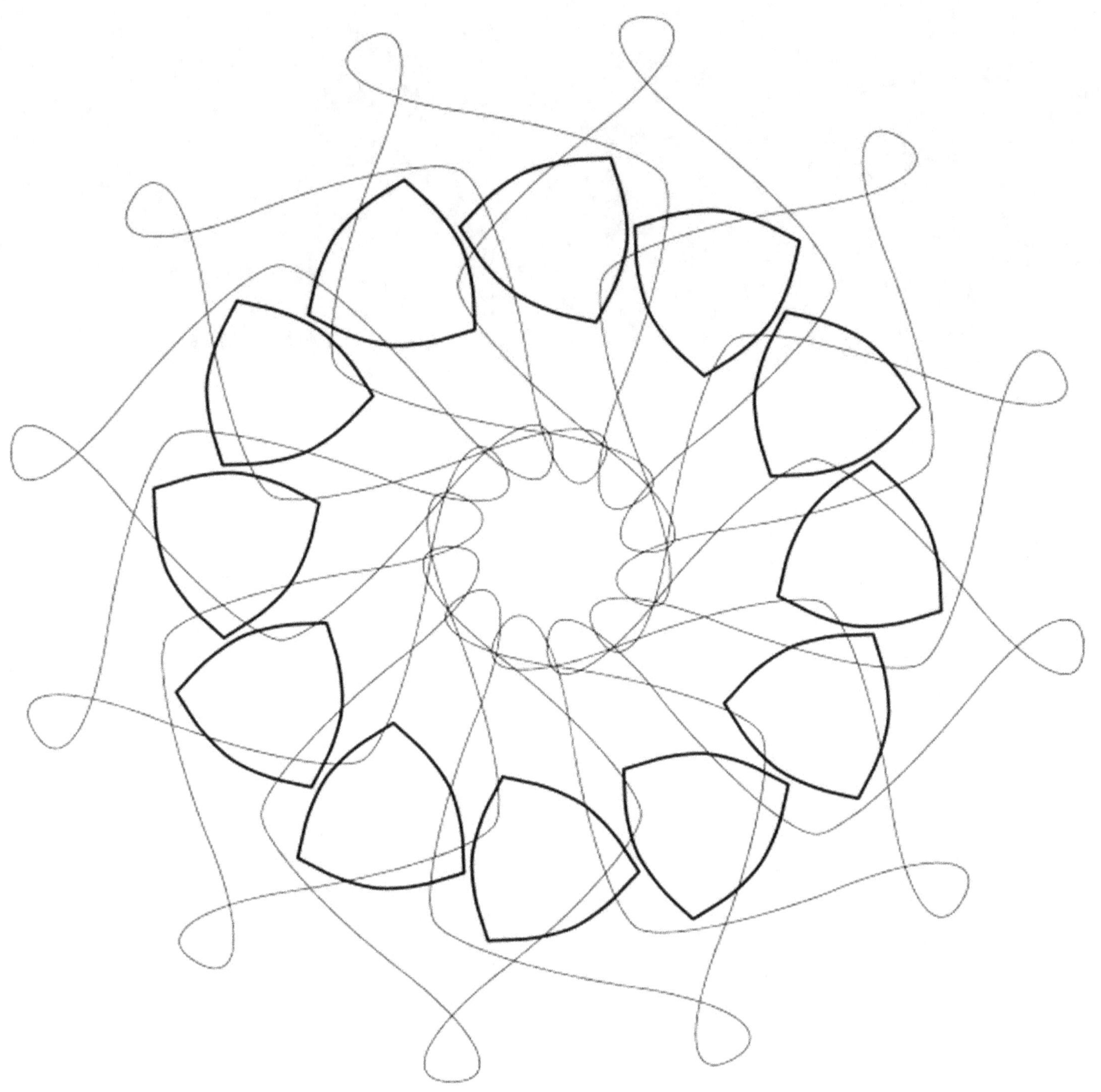

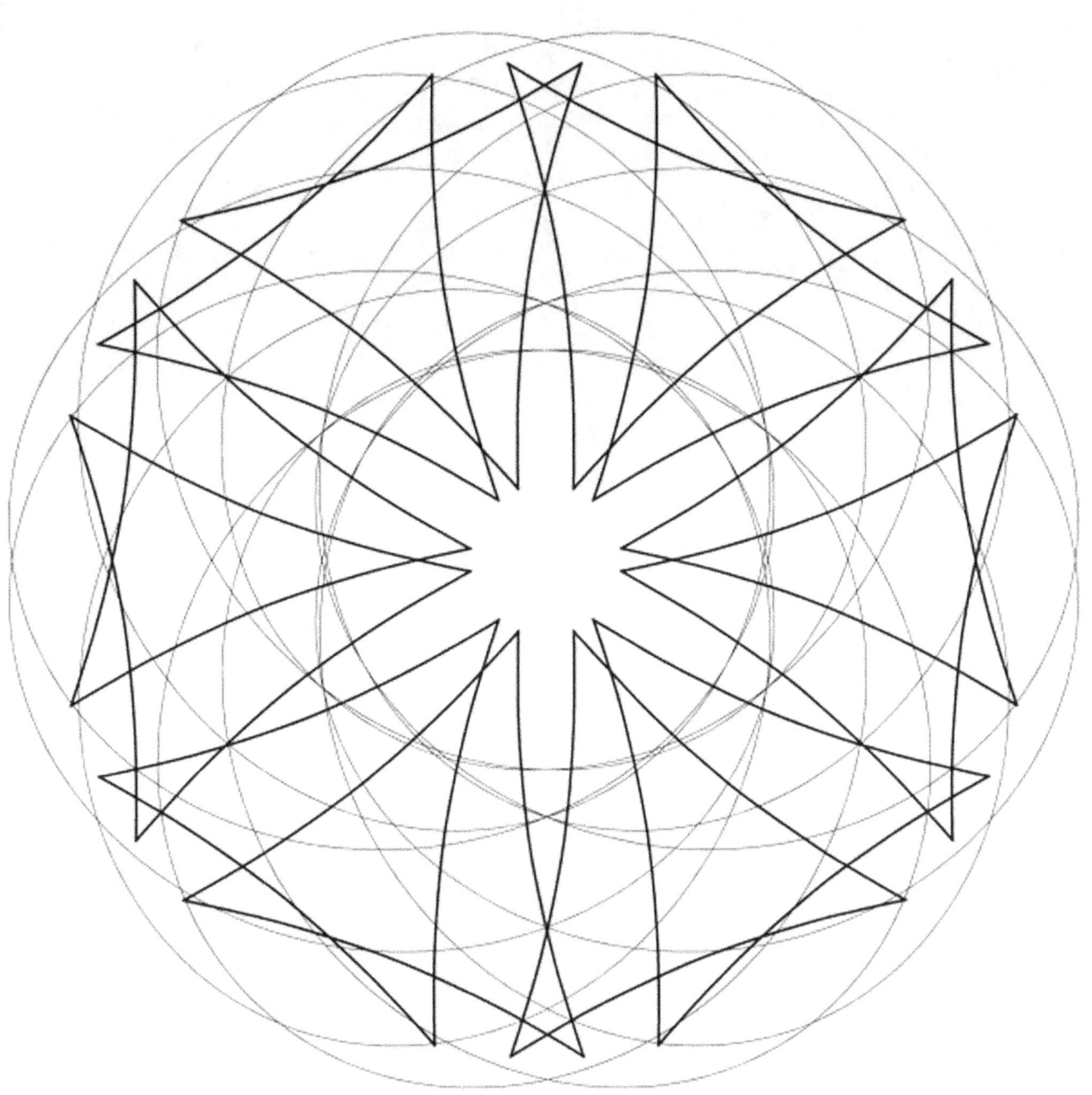

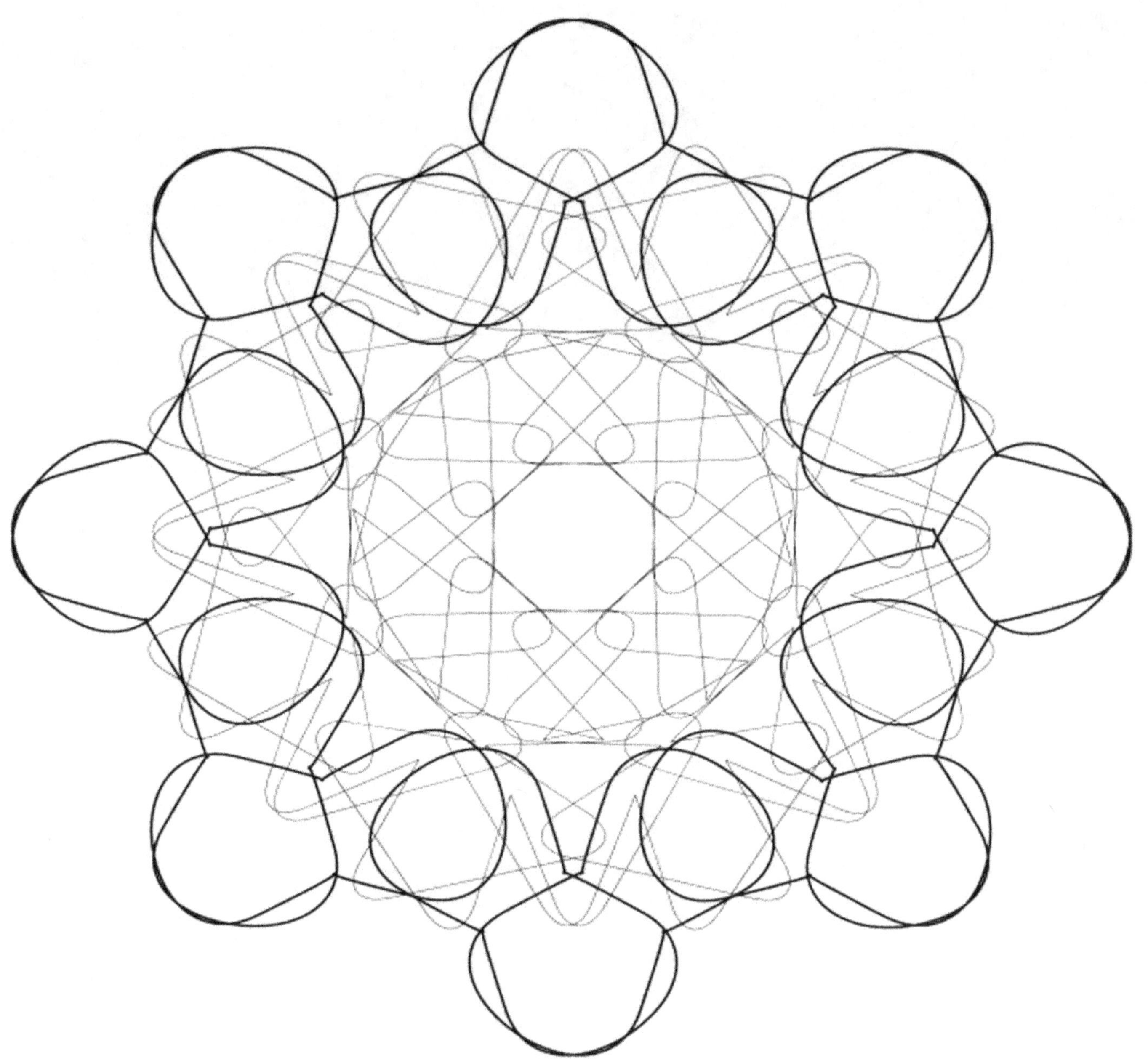

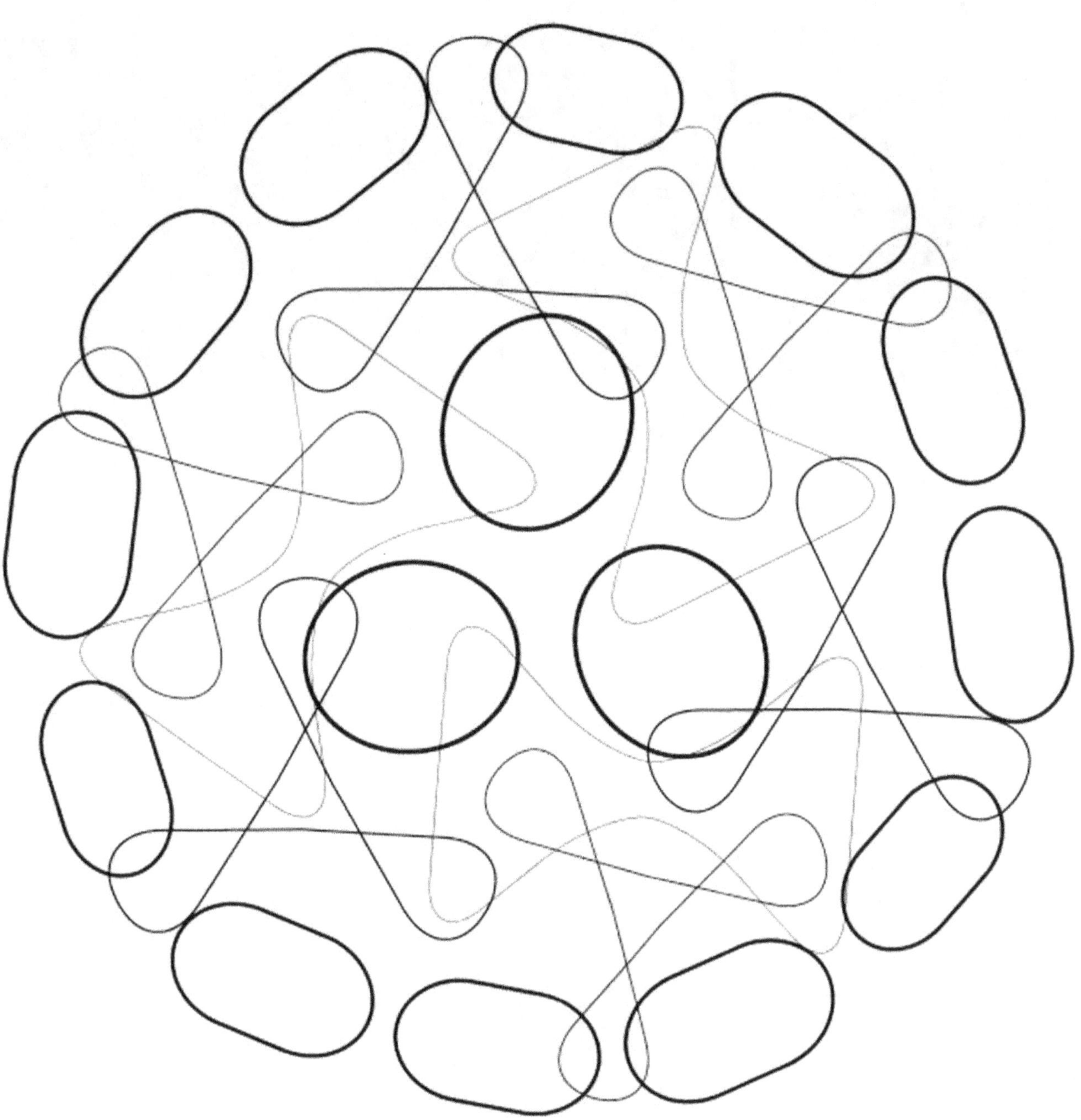

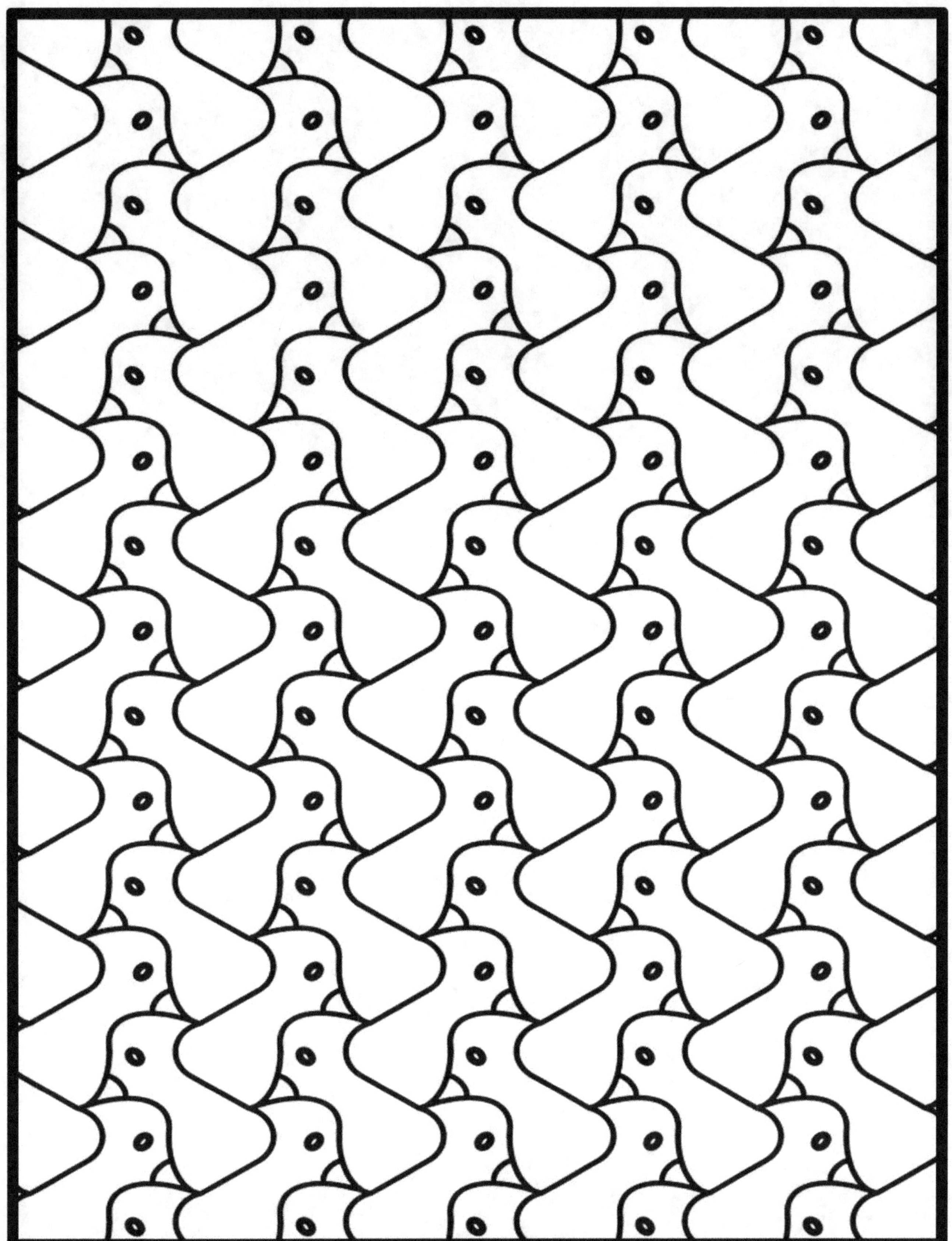

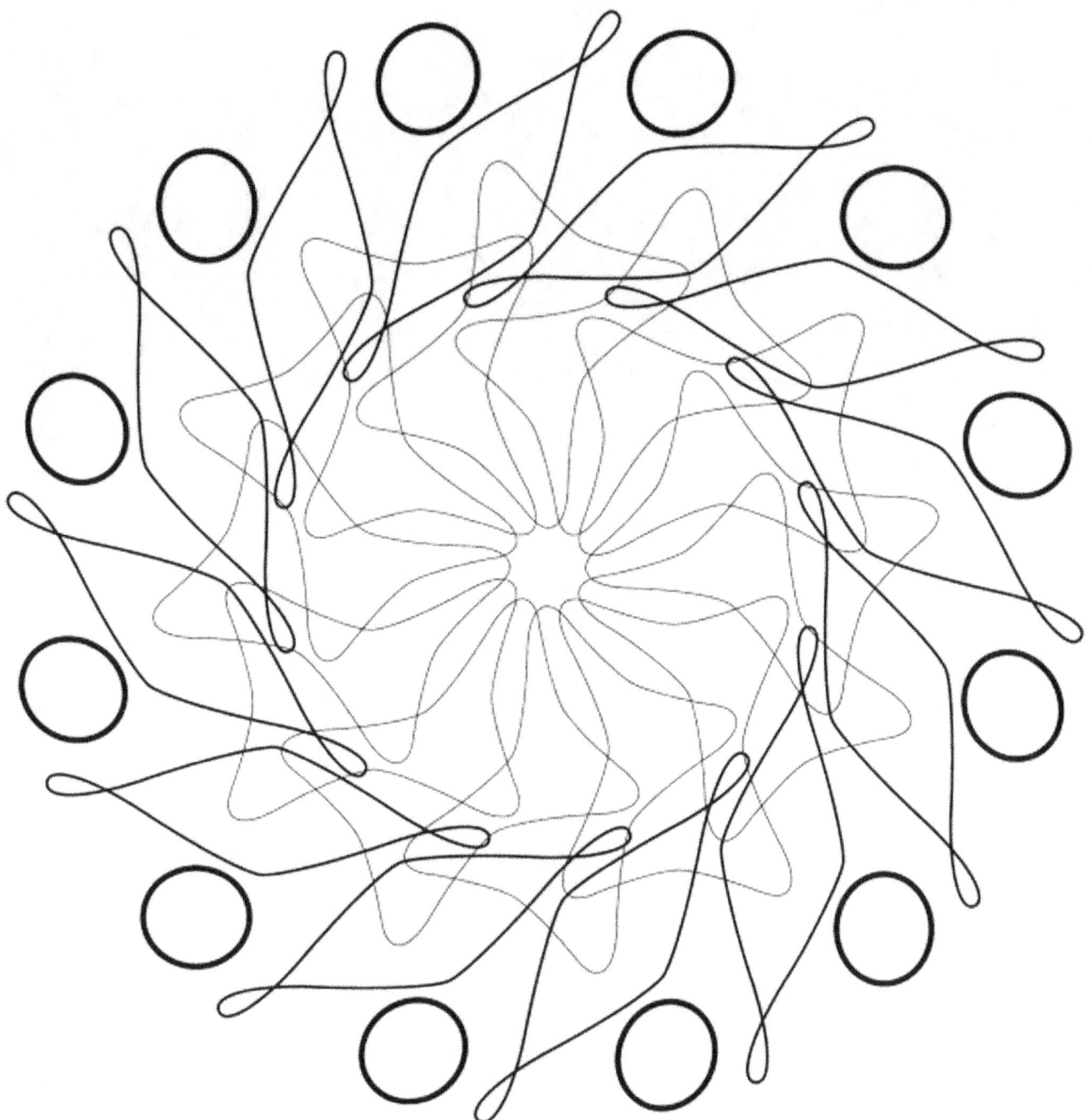